SPEAKING THROUGH MY SKIN

SPEAKING THROUGH MY SKIN

Poems by

Bruce A. Jacobs

Michigan State University Press
1996

All Michigan State University Press books are produced on paper which meets the requirements of American National Standards of Information Sciences— Permanence of paper for printed materials ANSI Z23.48-1984.

Michigan State University Press
East Lansing 48823

ISBN 0-87013-455-8

Lotus Poetry Series
Naomi Long Madgett, Editor

Grateful acknowledgment is given to the following publications in which some of the poems in this book have appeared:

African-American Review: "Church Lady," "Friendly Skies," and "The Neighborhood"; *Atlanta Review*: "For Sale"; *Green Fuse*: "Pissoir"; *GYST*: "Anchorage" and "Independence Day"; *Haight Ashbury Literary Journal*: "Hindsight"; *Many Mountains Moving*: "The Beer Joint" and "Masons"; *Obsidian II*: "Black on Black" and "Manners"; *Poets On: Coping*: "Lockjaw"; *Potato Eyes*: "Hypoxia"; and *The Pearl*: "Lost."

For Barry Kiener,
who insisted that I listen.

CONTENTS

I.

II.

III.

IV.

I.

LOCKJAW

While we work the brood mare barn,
Billy asks why all the band-aids.
I say something vague, not revealing
how much I like picking at scabs.

A doctor has warned me
it heightens risk of melanoma.
I can't help it. I want to go
back in time, peel the lie of thickened skin,
root in my own red flesh like swine,
come up with blood beneath my nails,
stain my clothes with memory.

To cover pain with skin, it seems to me,
is no great feat. Anyone with a scalpel
and time on their hands
can call themselves a healer.
But a fingernail: now that's an instrument
of God. One good furrow in the forearm,
worked deeply an hour a day, can stop the world,
grind back the push for closure.

I like to keep things open.
My flesh no longer winces.
With four or five good trenches going,
I've been in control since childhood.
The divorce, my father's eyes.
My landscape can support them.

I don't tell Billy this. We finish the stalls,
walk out back of the barn. He brings tools.

1

Now comes the part I like.
We grab pitchforks
and start digging.
Sharp and sure.

CLEANING FISH

He liked sex more than what came after:
small brown beings who
changed his lover's name to Mom,
roughened her doting hands and
robbed him of her gaze.
My sister learned to lie sweet nothings,
dodged his anger like a dancer.
I was heavy, could not run in water.

He convinced me that I did not like him,
that I was a little poacher. He would loom
in doorways, catching me always at it again,
stealing his space, while I hung pinned
like guilty meat in his barbed net.

So we sought out the gorge,
slid downward through scabbed shale,
the boulders harder than our fists,
the brown current louder than dinner talk,
the surrendered blood and scales wet and thick
on our skin, a prehistoric poultice
for the fever of our rage.

We made the climb back to the car
only when we had to,
swinging fresh corpses, smelling of battle
and smiling like two assassins.

THE BEER JOINT

It looked cool and dank
as the mouth of the stranger
we weren't supposed to talk to.
The darkness was dental,
a gnashing of tinkling glass
even at 10 a.m., and
I imagined that the hidden men within
all had bad breath and looked at women
with oddly moist appetites.

I'd pedal my bike to one edge
of the invisible line, then reverse
around the block to stop
at the other side.
We were forbidden to cross the doorway
and for me,
the monster in my closet
was enough.

FOUR BARS FOR BARRY
(for Barry Kiener)

"This is a blues." Three pained piano chords,
his eyes on me as if teaching the feel of a gun.
I'd never heard of music so deadly
as to deserve an article, the same way
he called out a Blakey triplet
as it shot past on vinyl,
or silenced me for the Coltrane sound.

I knew the zipper of a James Brown scream,
the way The Meters squared off the funk,
but this blue business of 12 or 16 bars,
diminished ninths, sounded too much
like work: a white boy's idea
of the purpose of my bones.
I said: Let's stick to fishing.

My mother remembers a sixth-grade assembly
where he was playing a funeral dirge
when the auditorium went pitch-black.
While janitors searched for fuses,
his hands found every tombstone,
fingers immune to darkness.
She still shakes her head.

I want to tell her to close her eyes,
imagine each key as life or death.

MASONS

Smug owners of
every parking space on my street after 7
they emerge from cars wielding dark suits,
tote black briefcases into the stone-toothed temple.

Their posture bears no hint of infanticide,
but their wing-tipped scuffle recalls
fraternity brother Dobson who, my father said,
terrorized our living room with His Goddamned Opinions.

It was all the same to me
from the shadows at the top of the stairs:
warm mutterings of scholarships and cotillions
wafting like cigar smoke
from the assembled brethren,
clink of glasses and flatware,
sounds of my mother's pies shrinking
to school lunch-box size amid laughing clamors
for her hand in marriage.

I would only hear of the carnage
much later, through their bedroom wall,
my father padding barefoot,
invoking the name like that of the Hydra:

"Dobson!"

A word that could grind a man
back to lost flesh, skinless boy
stripped too early, his own stolen father buried
in these deep and taunting voices.

Another evening with Dobson,
Another brotherhood of honking dark cars,
Another night with no place to park.

Behind Her Garage Seems Safe:

window frosted, today's trash out,
dead rosebushes for cover.
I light up and shiver, a 40-year-old man
hiding cigarettes from his mother,
jacket open to upstate December,
whipped clean of evidence by wind.

We all hide in turn. Me, my back to cinder block,
freeing held breath. After dark, raccoons,
stealthy as hogs, upending cans for drumsticks.
Beneath the flat-tired wheelbarrow, toads and slugs.
They tell me I should smoke, let it rust,
stop making work of secrets.
So does Sam, who's been dead ten years.
Against the fence next to his grave,
the sycamore I split and stacked one summer
rots into chain link smoothly as wet ashes.

Still, she could appear with new garbage,
catch me inhaling, drop the bag,
demand an answer about the wheelbarrow.
I could even head it off, stroll inside,
toss Marlboros onto her coffee table.
But then I'd have to ask her what she craves
besides cookies, and why she nearly slapped my sister
for broaching sex after the divorce.

Better to hunker in bramble,
count slowly toward 100, knowing only that someday,
after we've divided furniture, sold her house,
somebody's going to dig up that dog.

8

PARTY

What I remember is
the untouched M&Ms
in the bowl of that
empty room.
I had put out the word
for days: "Party at
my place. My Mom's away,"
imagining the white girls
who would not date me
and the clumping afroed bros
and sugar sisters
now dropping their sneers
to bump in the sweet smoke
of my family's proper dining room
and mouth to one another over the noise,
"Hey, we never knew
he was so *cool*."

Sometime after 11
the doorbell rang.
Jeff Stephens stepped in alone,
stood awkwardly
in the vacant red light
and tried to smile.
"Want some M&Ms?" I finally asked,
gesturing at the bowl.
"No thanks," he said
and left.

For Sale

"Just Divorced," reads the window sign.
"The judge says everything must be sold."

Tables, chairs, skillets, plates,
margarita glasses, strings of pearls,
a belly dancer's shimmy chain,
Bill Cosby records, all lined up
at one-time-only prices and I wish
my parents had known to do this,
cash in early, hand-paint a sign,
summon the neighborhood to settle this thing,

the bed that absorbed my father's lies
stripped to the mattress, price-tagged on the porch,
stacked photo frames sponged clean,
innocent as cafeteria trays,
our car priced to move, sold and gone
before it could carry perplexed children
on outings with his mistresses,
the house set free as lumber,
its hauntings swept to wind,

my parents warmly shaking hands, dividing the proceeds
of our family's better years
and handing each child a large check
with which we could run and shop
for anything,
anything we wanted.

REWIND

It hangs here
against the current: his voice,
dated days before the stroke,
before he thrashed on the carpet
for hours, before tiny catfish
burst out of his veins,

it hangs here. A protest carried
downstream. A voice on tape
insisting: "This is your father."

FAST FORWARD

"I'll meet you with the car," I say.
He turns, wheels himself one-handed,
every tile of hospital linoleum
a slope against his bleeding brain,
his gray head older, further off with
each stroke of chrome-spoked wheels,

already on trajectory,
knowing he will beat me there
without looking back.

FAMILY REUNION
(for Mary)

Call it deep as gardening,
the knowledge to carve a window
out of asphalt with keen brown hands,
sacrifice long fingernails
to ventilate the earth's desire.

Call it the sense of one's own flesh,
rampant as loam, sloughing concrete,
humming beneath every yard in the city,
uniting all fences and sidewalks,
one great and leafy laugh.

Call it something in the blood,
the way, beneath oaks in August,
two strangers gather acorns
and talk about the Family.

VIVIAN, TAKE 57

Cousin Vivian stayed single
all the 60 years we loved her,
and when she died,
in-laws from Philadelphia claimed her:
costume pearls, a thousand LPs
from Ellington to Coltrane,
velour couch, enameled bedroom set.
Blue shag.
They guarded their booty
right up through the funeral.

But,
What do you want of Vivian's?
hissed my mother
as we balanced Vivian's porcelain
on our laps, piled with turkey and dressing.
While kinfolk jabbed corn, dabbed eyes,
my mother's hands worked crowded rooms,
crammed a large purse with our past.

I remembered Vivian barking, "Base hit!"
at TV, cutting her words like the with-it cats
from Detroit who moved beneath crooked hats.
She knew the nod to walking bass,
spoke saxophone in days of Donna Reed,
was hipper even than my Uncle Wilbur
with his hi-fi and whitewalled T-bird.

Vivian, my secret beatnik, in her dietitian's lipstick,
pecking my round cheek with What's Cookin', Baby?
feeding me Oreos, then Miles Davis.
In the deep groove of her den,
all other relatives were squares.

From the days I called Tchaikovsky's 1812
"The Boom Song," we sat together,
our one face to the music.

At her funeral, I was thirty-two, unmarried,
did not cry. Until the bundle opened
in my hand: two little ivory elephants
wrapped in a napkin by my mother,
a woman who would steal
only for love or hunger.

II.

SECOND OPINION

I want a burglar who will take it all:
television, potted plants, notebooks,
but then return the stanzas
stripped, tightened, with a note
saying he won't press charges.

Give me the gift of theft.
I could use an appraisal
without a vested interest.
Make me buy back my belongings
until I recognize them.
Like the time a kid yelled "Nigger":
I clenched ancestry in my hands
more tightly than my grocery change.

Be the stranger who cards the lock,
turns the iron on while I'm on vacation,
rearranges furniture, surveys my rooms
like looking up a woman's dress.
Show no mercy through my windows.
Make razor-clean intrusions,
assault by stolen glimpses.

Kick in my door,
then report back to me.

THE THIRD DEGREE

No. I didn't ask the reason.
He said he needed theft.
I take work where I can get it.
Sure, it was unusual. Most people
want their televisions.
But this guy had a problem.
He'd forgotten what he owned,
said he needed to start clean.
I've seen this before. My cellmate
in Coxsackie was a painter.
He'd sell canvasses to rich people,
break into their houses with turpentine.

The poem? That was an accident.
He'd left it on the counter.
I took one look, dropped the silverware,
went searching for red ink.
I've never pulled a gun on a job
but that sonnet had to die.
I promised him I wouldn't talk
if he'd abandon verse.
Okay, okay. So we both lied.

Look, it's a service business.
The customer is always right.
If seeing "Sony," "Oster," "Pyrex"
makes him forget his name,
then I've got work to do.
I can't let his pain stop me;
there's no way out but surgery.
Thirty-odd years of "Yes, I'll take it,"
TVs, blenders lodged against his spine.
He could hardly walk. He wept with relief
after I fenced the stuff.

That's all I know. Except he called again last week.
Probably another sonnet.

HANGING JUDGE

Three robberies before lunch,
and now this.
Victim pleading guilty,
burglar begging innocence,
stolen durables no one wants to claim,
bad sonnets placing both men at the scene.

A body would at least be proof
of what this man has lost.
Instead he stands here ranting
about murder by television.
Release him? He'll be back next week
with whoever's caught selling his clothes.
Then reporters, TV anchors,
stories about the judge
who let a man be robbed of everything.

What happened to the days
when people simply bought new wallets
and thieves were self-employed?
It's always artists. People without wallpaper.

But sonnets are a start. Ten syllables of labor
will teach a man to put his house in order,
show a skulking editor where to keep his hands.

I sentence you each to consecutive terms.
Any funny stuff with rhyme schemes
and you're looking at hard time.

TAKING THE FIFTH

We plot capers in our cages,
etch floor plans in concrete:
he leads me through alarms,
I show him how to be invisible.
When guards approach, the trusty whistles,
we pull out Collected Works.

Halfway through *Othello*,
we come up with the big one.
We start small, with sonnets,
practice on our cell block.
Soon we can hold a man captive
with standard English meter.
Then lyric verse. The judge was right.
All attention strains for order.
Two months and the guards are zombies,
the warden wants to talk.

By the time we get to long poems
we know the world is ours.
We have found what oils the air,
what turns the wheel of breathing.
Night watchmen will be helpless.
Bank guards will stare like jacklit deer.
One of us will wield the verse,
the other lift the goods.
We'll head west, job to job,
hit libraries for ammo.

The best part is, no evidence.
We'll memorize the poems.
If we get caught, we know nothing.
We're part of the public domain.

THE NEIGHBORHOOD

I hear their days and nights
as screeching tires and sirens,
people skidding without plans or mortgages,
breathing hard between buses, landlords,
late checks, impatient cops,
suspicious clerks, social workers, long lines.

I lie in bed, hear them laugh late nights
at the dumb luck of lineage, as I
laugh at the rich who totter into inheritance.

I live a punctuation, a movement of intervals
recognized in dictionaries and therapy
but not in front of the funeral home.
A young boy asks me a detailed question
and I understand not one word.

Our brownness is but shared air.

MAGIC

Makes no sense. This late at night,
a little girl in sneakers wielding
a stick? Three feet of hollow prod, alley bamboo,
one wooden tap and each kid runs.
Crazy is contagious.

She flaunts the wand like dime-store jewelry,
treasure of the moment, trigger-ready
in case of need for sorcery as they pass by my stoop,
knowing I could be anybody, hands in my pockets like that.
Her brown face bolts at me, pops me with a "Hi!"
They billow laughter up the street:
"You talked to him   talked to that man   you so bold."

It's crazy. Taking potions literally,
casting my bones on sooted marble,
believing bulrushes can push through concrete
and shelter babies left in alleys.
I want to tell her that her world
is reed and stone. She ought to
learn construction. One cannot trust
the way things work in moonlight.

It's crazy. Making games with strangers,
playing where she's not supposed to,
a black girl shaking giggle sticks into the night.

LOST

help, she is wailing,
help, from the pavement, help,
from her knees, but her purse is gone,
he is all legs and sneakers, over the hedge,
and she is broken heels and torn hose
and scraped skin in a smart checkered suit and it is
gone, the walking free of larger hands,
gone, the swinging of her arms, gone,
the unclutched rhythm of her pendulum, and she flails
breached in birth from cracked concrete
this world a sidewalk in her wet face,
her mouth moving its small help, help,
a grown woman in ripped black stockings
kneeling blind in sunlight while silhouettes
sift past, none bending close to breathe
it's all right
she will learn to live here
it's all right
she bleeds salt on the tarmac
it's all right
she rises, peeling rock from skin
as her eyes search for home.

CHURCH LADY

High heels and red beret
are her earthly parentheses.
She hums a hymn
of sidewalk mercy,
ascending past my smile.

In my leather and my languor
she may see sin on a stoop,
but it's all right.
She does not know she saved my life the night
a fistful of lost boys held their anger
to my head, filled the alley with a cannon,
promised me that they would use it,
and later, deciding my money would not do,
edged me into a garage
to finish things in darkness.

But then her Lord appeared
in sudden incandescent light, the back door
of the church flying open, spilling pilgrims
into the night, where they stood bearing witness
to this trial, the boys caught now
in smiting brightness, frozen
in the judging moment
before fleeing back to shadow.

As she passes on this Sunday
in her hat and heels,
done up in articles of faith
beyond the reach of sidearms,

she clutches her church within herself,
does not return my smile.

So many souls to save.
Too many faces to remember.

BARTER

He finds himself
at my stone steps,
looks up to ask Can I get a cigarette?
I tell him Sorry, it's my last one.
He says Then can I share it with you?
I say No. He says I'll pay you. I say No.
He smiles harder,
says Man, I just walked
from Park Heights. I'm desperate.
Let me buy it short off you. Give you a dollar.
I say No.

He sputters, shakes his head, walks off.
We are two black men. I should know the rest:
In 1620 he lost his power to create,
and now he needs a cigarette.
What's he supposed to do?

He looks back at me,
shouts, Five hundred dollars!

This is when I know we share
an expensive habit.

PISSOIR

All of the politics
come down to this:
there is no place to piss
on the street.

All urinals are locked
behind silent insistences
that you purchase things
stroll aisles as a customer
now entitled to relief
or pass invited into
some abode where you can
excuse yourself among friends.

Pissing is not a right
but a privilege
bought with grocery change,
bottomless coffee or
small talk in living rooms.

Being in a strange neighborhood
in this country
renders one homeless
to find an alley,
undo your zipper and
think of Paris.

MENTORING

"Being black," he told me,
between mouthfuls of vegetarian barbecue,
"is not as easy as you think.
You ought to work at doing it my way."

"You mean," I asked,
"be proudly ignorant and bitter
instead of proudly proud,
rattle shackles like jewelry,
wear kente like a black cross
instead of like a robe of rainbows,
seek out chips to shoulder in fear of nakedness,
collect brochures of Africa but never maps,
pretend that your friends and
your found neighborhood are our new nation,
shout whenever possible,
read nothing that does not come from your experience,
misunderstand the Zulu, define the Middle Passage
as the start or end of history,
walk always under palm trees because
you cannot remember,
refuse to learn to spell,
view English as a minefield,
write the same praise poem 100 times, 200,
whatever it takes to recover from who you are,
see musicals entitled 'Momma My Foot Hurts'
and feel your greatness consummated,
call all noise redemption, celebrate only in safety,

chant against the other, mistake familiarity for family,
seek mediocrity as success at discount prices,
make only easy movements,
know only what you know?"

"Exactly," he replied.
"There may be hope for you yet."

III.

Summer Before I Took the S.A.T.

What I didn't know
as we licked purple windowpane,
dissolved our heads on patios,
my white friends couldn't tell me:

that I would want those brain cells back
the year I learned I had to be
smarter than my boss
to land the job beneath him.

SHE WAS JUST AS BLOND

as in high school. But now,
she drove an 18-wheeler.
She said she'd met a trucker
who wanted to make music.
They'd struck a deal:
she taught him piano,
he taught her diesel mechanics.

I didn't say,
"Instead of dumping me junior year,
you could have shown me
where your racist grandfather
kept his razor.
Then I could have shown you
how to avoid the beatings."

INDEPENDENCE DAY

I want to take a rowboat ride
with Francis Scott Key,
some drunken pub song in my belly,
rollicking in the midnight red glare
with those brass-band drum bombs bursting in air,
a six-pack in the gunwale,
oarlocks clanking like empty glasses,
thinking, this could be a holiday
maybe in July, we could
light the sky, drink warm beer,
ruffle the water with heroic lies
but never tell of this, our blowout of black waves
and heady foam, Frank and I
pulling a tab for every rocket
drinking to new countries and old girlfriends
bugger off the Queen and her bastard offspring
in God we trust.
No one else will be invited.
This will be our party.

Thirty Years After Watching "Johnny Quest" on TV Every Saturday Morning

I want to come as a cartoon vision
to baffled, loinclothed Caucasians,
bring fire to blue-eyed forest people
who cringe like bowling pins.
I want to tour with a blond valet named "Race"
who flies my daddy's private plane,
have a pious white-boy sidekick
who answers faithfully to "Howdy,"
never laughs too loudly,
saves my small dog from quicksand.

I want to swoop down by jet-pack
on Rotary Club meetings, break up evil sacrifice,
send pink natives running for sedans.
I want to rout pale-faced cannibal cults
to a soundtrack of Charlie Parker triplets,
their eggshell eyes wide as China,
cringing like gophers at the foot
of a shrine to Mel Tormé.

I want to safari behind picket fences,
free poodles wrapped in old chains,
lead them in legion to Little League fields,
allow freckled lackeys to shoulder my baggage,
follow me to a nook of linoleum,
serve me bowls of crunchy-sweet cereal,
tremble and genuflect at my blue screen
until I smile through my thick glasses,
hold out my urn of Sugar Crisp
and bid them all rise
to call me Bwana.

I want cream-faced boys on Saturdays
to open mouths to TV screens,
to lift spoons to my visage,
to hunger six days of creation
for one half-hour of Sabbath,
thirty animated minutes
when I invent the world.

AFTER THE 200TH WHITE PERSON
LOCKS HER CAR DOOR AT ME

Makes me wish
my distant cousin
had told the first of them
on the West shore:

"No. This isn't Africa.
Head due south
until you hit ice.
You can't miss it."

MANNERS

We stand here, watching marchers
make work of dance. What does that make us?
A moving memory of days
when Crazy Horse need never preach
that people were not made to work,
a roundness squeezed through quadrants,
seeking motion without corners,
journeying Delta furrows, long steel rails
and concrete grids carved like tunnels
beneath our open history.

They build walls to construct freedoms,
and how are we to hold our knowledge
that we have tried all of this before,
that kings are only tools of singing?

If we could grab their square bone shoulders,
shove drums into their bellies,
make them feel heartbeats through their spines,
then they might know how to move in vastness.

But how do you teach the movement of air,
the rhythm of silence, the meaning
of a world's work already done?

FRIENDLY SKIES

Her smile durable as chrome,
she moves seamlessly up the aisle,
courting untold closeness with
200 of the nicest people she has ever met.
She could be my great-grandmother at 25,
quick with coffee over banquets
where a black woman could not sip,
tall cotton waiting as her thanks for affability.

I watch for stress lines, metal fatigue,
a cracking at the corners of the lipstick
but she is just the way I want her:
in love with blind acquaintance,
each offering of her hand a moment's wedding,
each gesture gently powdered with romance.
And by the time she gets to me with
        "Soft drink? Peanuts?"
I am as certain of what she means
as any guest at a plantation.

In a steel tube above the clouds,
a man can believe anything.

OVERHEARD

"Can you see yourself married?" he asks.
She pets her dog, says,
"Authentically, no. But I did it
for fourteen years, inauthentically.
It wasn't my authentic self."

Leading me to wonder
if all of that licking and wagging
is her dog's authentic self
or if it's the collar talking,
supple ring of this strange marriage.

TRIAL SEPARATION

We are being good to ourselves.
We are rediscovering each other.
Picking our voices out of a crowd.
Swallows and salmon work this way;
a thousand salty miles is just far enough
to know the lure of that one rafter
or bed of smooth stones.

The phone book looks thinner already.
I start with AA Cleaners and Dyers, ask them
what you do when you've bought a woman an ironing board
and she tells you to stop looking at her clothes.
They say she came in for help just last week
but the creases will come out only with wear.

By the time I get to the D's, I have learned
that she traded in the car for bus fare,
returned perfume to a tulip nursery,
exchanged the vacuum cleaner for a lawn spreader.
The receipts litter the entire Mid-Atlantic coast.
Getting to know her is more work than I thought.

The day I sell my furniture to pay my phone bill
I have made it through the R's. I can feel her getting closer.
At SOS Scrap Metal & Salvage, a man answers,
tells me I just missed her:

She brought in an ironing board, two hundred wire hangers,
looked as if she was dressed for the ocean.

IV.

DARK ALLEYS
(for E. E. M.)

Smooth as a detective the way he tells me
that this is never gunplay;
the heat between the shoulder blades
when he calls me "Negro" on the phone
is laughter. A friend at my back.

Blood comes too easily to ex-slaves, he says.
What if instead we took our pulse as music?
We could bless the turbulence of our skins,
feel gratitude for brown rivers,
weep in our own dark water,
smile at our own nature —

— the way private eyes
sit with their backs to doorways,
savor the possibilities.

MAN OF STEEL

It is not the way I'd like to die:
two shots through the skull
with the blunt end of a Buck knife.
The fish mouths silent vowels in the sink
while my neighbor hovers, telling me
about her car being broken into,
a U-Haul sucking her house clean
of roommates, her awakening alone
on a hundred thirty acres
with all the mares sold and gone
and last year's rape lingering
in the downstairs bedroom air.

She has the same first name as my girlfriend,
says she wants to watch me clean the fish.
I disembowel nicely,
thumbnail hard along the spine,
but I've botched the clubbing.
The fishy mouth still moves in our faces
like a bad ventriloquist.
She stares at it in fascination,
asks me if it's dead.
I mumble something about autonomic nerves,
which I have never understood.

She wants to know how long I'll stay
before returning to the city,
if Thursday she can come and do her wash.
The fish keeps interrupting her.
I cut off its head,
but its mouth will not stop moving.
It mocks our conversation
the way that ghosts knock over vases.

When my girlfriend takes the elevator
to do laundry, I sometimes worry.
There is a man some floors above
who talks crazy.
I whack the severed head again.
It makes no difference.
The fish insists.
My neighbor tries to ignore it.

The beheaded bass works its jaws,
contradicting me as I tell her
Thursday is fine and
if she is ever nervous on these nights,
I'll be here to help.

WHILE THE RADIO WARNED
OF IMMINENT WAR

He had hidden all the kitchen knives, he said,
before he told his wife about Cecelia's skin.
It was not that he had slept with her,
but that he hadn't, that her mere touch
cut him to the bone. I said I thought

I'd have a fish sandwich on a bun, french fries,
food I could get my hands around with no utensils.
He ordered only ice cream, shoveled sweetness
while relating the worst week of his life.
Of course, it is by now a cliché

to order a fish sandwich and fries with ketchup.
But I like the familiar. Some things you just accept:
the way a square fish without tail might swim,
the years spent spooling her wet hair off the soap.
But even monofilament, clothesline, twine

can end a marriage. He had hidden them, as well,
before returning to their bed. He felt
his neck led nowhere, leaving all love nameless.
You don't know what this is like, he said.
I bit into my fish sandwich. This was some months

before the night my girlfriend wept to me
about being attracted to another man
and I told her of my flirtation with an artist.
We clutched each other like diseased newlyweds,
our immunity falling like scales. I knew one thing:

My sandwich was good. We paid our check.
I looked at him and wondered if some year
I myself might find nutrition pointless,
ice cream as good a late lunch with a friend
as any other.

HYPOXIA

Ellen calls one evening
to tell of a friend's iguana
that fell victim to the cat.

Somehow the cage lid came off.
Nobody saw it happen.
They found the lizard,
all four legs chewed off,
blinking at them.

The husband said put it
in the sink, under a brick,
submerged in water.
Their little boy was crying.
Couldn't they save it? They could
call the vet. Do an operation.
Her husband took the boy upstairs.
After fifteen minutes underwater,
the iguana lay in her hands,
blinked at her again.

She called Ellen in a panic.
What should she do?
Her son was hysterical.
This could mean therapy.
Could a lizard be put to sleep?
But that seemed ridiculous.
Ellen suggested a blunt object.
Her friend said maybe. She didn't know.
This was so horrible.
She'd call her back.

The next day the friend told Ellen
she had finally wrapped the lizard
in two plastic bags, put it
in the trash, gone to bed.
In the morning it was dead.
Her son held the funeral.

Ellen and I share an awful laugh,
then hang up without speaking
of how the two of us no longer breathe
together.

I lie blinking at my ceiling,
the night like tight black plastic.

HINDSIGHT

She filled that cotton blouse like billowed curtains
and smiled such a front-porch dare
that I failed to read her eyes
or even those shiny stickers
with slogans like "I Am A Good Person!"
and "Tomorrow Is Another Day"
lining the inside of her car
like a repair-shop waiting room
while she doctored me with
natural cosmetics from her sample case.

She had beaten cancer, she told me.
All I knew was I had never
kissed a woman more alive,
her lips like small and greedy hands,
our clothes loosening like steaming skin
in my hotel room, when suddenly
she went cold, dropped
her arms from me like anvils,
stammered apologies of
Just Too Difficult and
Not Being Ready,
then fled as from a fire, fighting
zippers and buttons through the door.

Blurred nights later, I awakened
to a vision of a woman falling toward swords
through hotel air cold as isopropyl alcohol,
her blouse pulled about her like a shield
against the hope that I might be the one

to caress her new parentheses,
read stories in her spaces,
dare to kiss the skin
next to her heart.

ANCHORAGE

The mountains ring downtown like teeth
of some buried necklace marking this ground
with earthen ceremony.
The concrete feels thin, even
on Fourth Street, where a drunken Eskimo
spars on the curb with steel totems
and a white woman in an orange bellbottom pantsuit
billows through 1967.
The jewelry is for tourists,
scrimshaw and holy beads
carved and strung in Korea
by hands that have never cut ice,
but it pays rent, feeds memory.

In the center of town, Earthquake Park
is fenced off like a rash,
its houses broken scabs,
the ground heaved with allergic fits,
scratched raw, blood dried in chasms.

The city mascot is a tame caribou,
but the outdoor cage is empty.
"He's dead," the guy tells me.
"People sneak by at night
and shoot 'em."

Soon, he says,
they'll have another.

MAKEOVER

Now it shows even in the mirror.
I'm made of cement, each tiny spiked stone
glued into place against protest.
They say this kind of friction is bad for the skin
though a mason might call it a good bond.
My cells bind on themselves, a wall with me in it,
platelets of earth that immerse me like bath water.

In the next room, Ellen laughs long-distance
on the phone, her happiness
loud as construction.
She has a child's complexion,
tells me now that we live together
I'll see her evenings in facial mask.

I don't tell her I've seen her secret
in France, where they peel decades off cathedrals
every 50 years with steam, shield beauty
with materials mixed by heat and time.
On the Ile de Saint Louis in Paris,
a man can scrape his skin to pulp on granite,
slosh amid crowds like spilled wine
safely cupped in stone.

If only the road crew outside the window
would stop that grinding. I'd turn away,
call from the bathroom, ask Ellen
to help me find my face in clay.

DARK HORSE

Two mornings after Billy and I
lose a hundred dollars at the track,
I see Leroy about my hair.
He stares out of the empty barber shop
at sidewalks of untrimmed black men.

He nods toward the deli across the street,
says he's giving up red meat,
that life of drugs and hormones.
His head is ashen, gray as mine
before he put me onto Just For Men,
the natural hair color that's easy on the scalp.

This isn't the Leroy who told a roomful of old heads
how his wife laughed at him inking his hair
after he'd packed his bags for a trip.
What good was the dye, she asked him,
if he didn't do his pubic hair, too?
What he didn't tell her, he grinned, was that he had.
The vinyl chairs made us laugh harder.

That was last summer, before the African boutique
and record shop next door went broke.
Leroy lowers the cape onto me. The radio is off.
On the VCR, Minister Louis Farrakhan is saying
he does not hate white skin,
only the color of evil. I wonder if he dyes his hair.
My roots are sprouting silver. But I feel lucky,
tell Leroy to cut it short.

By the next morning, I'm back in the shower
with a bottle of Leroy's brand of black.
Whoever makes this stuff has been to the races,
understands the way a bettor
wants to take the numbers in his hands,
run with fate like a three-year-old
no track has ever seen. It's our secret
that I'm a guy who turns 40 in April.
The dye splatters, stings my eyes
like blinding sweat on a contender.

I check results in the mirror:
head of thick black hair. But wait.
Beneath, dark circles ring my eyes
in matching Natural Jet Black
where the dye took to tender skin.
Now I'm not even an aging Appaloosa.
I'm a 39-year-old raccoon.
Worse, the tub and toilet seat
are stained like ceramic Dalmatians.
I ask Ellen if I look stupid. She says no,
but she sounds like Fernando Lamas:
It is better to feel like an idiot
than to look like an idiot.
Her makeup won't help. It's too light.
Maybe peroxide around the eyes.

Three days ago, it seemed like a good idea:
30-to-1 odds after Danette's horse took a spill
in the tacking paddock, a grandstand full of suckers
looking at accident instead of bloodlines.
We'd learn later that it was not her horse,
that a scratched filly had changed the lineup,
making the Number 8 mare somebody else's:

a nag that would carry our cash
down the lane dead last.

BLACK ON BLACK

1.
Night street an onyx eye unblinking, empty
but for him, black man, hood up,
coat too big, one hand deep in pocket.
Walks too fast, crossing toward me
I see now he's shaggy, 50 feet
and closing but still time for him
to look away, pull out a handkerchief,
too soon for me to jump to how
white people run from us.

Twenty feet, eyes in the hood are on me,
his angle sharper, no mistake,
watch the hand, watch the hand, still in
that big pocket, street is blind,
shuttered, faceless, look for escape,
see small yard with gate,
close my hand on mace.

Ten feet and he has not shaved, the parka is blue
with tattered fur, the hand is shoved to hell
down that huge pocket, in five seconds he will
draw forth flame, in five seconds he will
withdraw magnetic steel and make me slave
to gravity, his eyes are pulling for me,
his mouth about to move, make things official.

Five feet and all sidewalk leads to him,
the hand now cranking from the pocket
like a steam shovel as his lips open,
the words will be the final kiss,
no time to mourn for lost brothers,
Move! I take the gate in three steps running,

make the yard, have gained 10 feet in snow
when his hand clears the pocket
to reveal a driver's license,
his ID, panhandling weapon against fear.

Not gonna rob you, sir, he says. Can you spare some change?

2.
Only after the elevator doors pinch off the night
does the attack come. I strike out, shout,
pound enameled walls for escape, but too late,
I am trapped in this bright cell
with a man who wears my clothes, jingles my keys
and spends our evenings
posing threats from doorway shadows,
holding soft lives hostage.
I have felt him follow me to entrances,
crossed streets against him,
scanned for him before parallel parking,
and handed him my wallet.
I have seen others shy from me
as from a disguised shark, shimmy past as if my hands
were hooks for women's purses.

Now here we are, two black men
within one skin, me alone in an elevator.
Me as the man who might have mugged me.
Me shoving myself against the wall,
blowing mirrors through my own brain.

IT'S A DOG'S LIFE

We all look at corpses
with the same impending knowledge.
We could give up now, say what's the use
when it all comes to nothing
but hands crossed in plumped silk,
pine bonfires,
the solvent of deep water.

And if this is but a vigil before glory,
why waste time? 70 years is too long
to wait for a bus. You could feel silly
learning bird songs,
chipping your skin toward love
only to declare at last,
"Oh. Here comes mine. The 32."

I say it's a dog's life:
We come when called for sustenance,
but moments have no names.